YET MORE POETIC GEMS

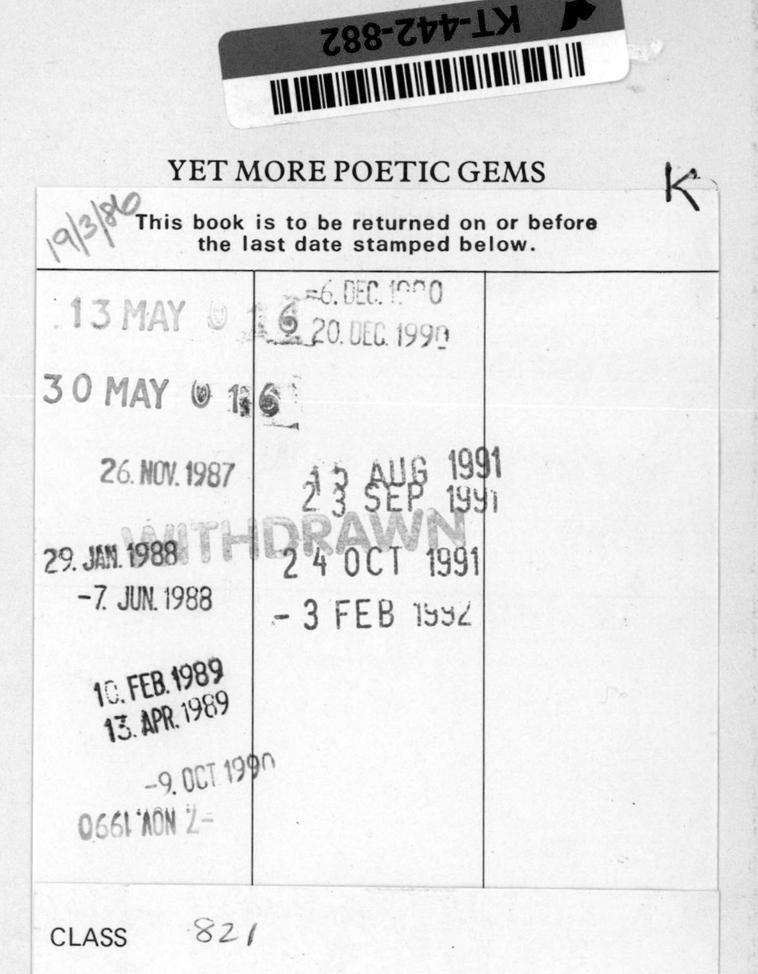

YET MORE POETIC GEMS

William McGonagall

Poet and Tragedian

Died in Edinburgh 29th September, 1902

DUCKWORTH

First published in this edition 1980

Gerald Duckworth & Co Ltd
The Old Piano Factory
43 Gloucester Crescent, London NW1

ISBN 0 7156 1511 4

Typeset by Elanders Computer Assisted
Typesetting Systems, Inverness
and printed and bound in Great Britain by
Redwood Burn Limited
Trowbridge and Esher

CONTENTS

SUMMARY HISTORY OF SIR WILLIAM WALLACE

Sir William Wallace of Ellerslie,
I'm told he went to the High School in Dundee,
For to learn to read and write,
And after that he learned to fight.
While at the High School in Dundee,
The Provost's son with him did disagree,
Because Wallace he did wear a dirk,
He despised him like an ignorant stirk,
Which with indignation he keenly felt,
And told him it would become him better in his belt.

Then Wallace's blood began to boil,
Just like the serpent in its coil,
Before it leaps upon its prey;
And unto him he thus did say:
"Proud, saucy cur, come cease your prate,
For no longer I shall wait,
For to hear you insult me,
At the High School in Dundee;
For such insolence makes my heart to smart,
And I'll plunge my dagger in your heart."

Then his heart's blood did quickly flow,
And poor Wallace did not know where to go;
And he stood by him until dead.
Then far from him he quickly fled,
Lamenting greatly the deed he had done,
The murdering of the Provost's son.

The scene shifts to where he was fishing one day,
Where three English soldiers met him by the way,
And they asked him to give them some fish,

And from them they would make a delicious dish.
Then Wallace gave them share of his fish,
For to satisfy their wish;
But they seemed dissatisfied with the share they got,
So they were resolved to have all the lot.

Then Wallace he thought it was time to look out,
When they were resolved to have all his trout;
So he swung his fishing-rod with great force round his head,
And struck one of them a blow that killed him dead;
So he instantly seized the fallen man's sword,
And the other two fled without uttering a word.

Sir William Wallace of Ellerslie,
You were a warrior of great renown,
And might have worn Scotland's crown;
Had it not been for Monteith, the base traitor knave,
That brought you to a premature grave;
Yes! you were sold for English gold,
And brought like a sheep from the fold,
To die upon a shameful scaffold high,
Amidst the derisive shouts of your enemies standing by.

But you met your doom like a warrior bold,
Bidding defiance to them that had you sold,
And bared your neck for the headsman's stroke;
And cried, "Marion, dear, my heart is broke;
My lovely dear, I come to thee,
Oh! I am longing thee to see!"
But the headsman was as stolid as the rock,
And the axe fell heavily on the block,
And the scaffold did shake with the terrible shock,
As the body of noble Wallace fell,
Who had fought for Scotland so well.

THE HEATHERBLEND CLUB BANQUET

'Twas on the 16th of October, in 1894,
I was invited to Inverness, not far from the seashore,
To partake of a Banquet prepared by the Heatherblend
Club,
Gentlemen who honoured me without any hubbub.

The Banquet was held in the Gellion Hotel,
And the landlord, Mr Macpherson, treated me right
well;
Also the servant maids were very kind to me,
Especially the girl who polished my boots most beautiful to
see.

The Banquet consisted of roast beef, potatoes, and red
wine,
Also hare soup and sherry, and grapes most fine,
And baked pudding and apples, lovely to be seen,
Also rick sweet milk and delicious cream.

Mr Gossip, a noble Highlander, acted as chairman,
And when the Banquet was finished the fun began;
And I was requested to give a poetic entertainment,
Which I gave, and which pleased them to their hearts'
content.

And for the entertainment they did me well reward
By entitling me the Heatherblend Club Bard;
Likewise I received an Illuminated Address,
Also a purse of silver, I honestly confess.

Mr A. J. Stewart was very kind to me,
And tried all he could to make me happy;
And several songs were sung by gentlemen there—
It was the most social gathering I've been in, I do declare.

Oh, magnificent town of Inverness!
With its lovely scenery on each side,
And your beautiful river, I must confess,
'Twould be good for one's health there to reside.

There the blackbird and the mavis doth sing,
Making the woodland with their echoes to ring;
During the months of July, May and June,
When the trees and shrubberies are in full bloom.

And to see the River Ness rolling smoothly along,
Together with the blackbird's musical song;
As the sun shines bright in the month of May,
'Twill help to drive dull care away.

And Macbeth's Castle is grand to be seen,
Situated on Castle Hill, which is beautiful and green,
'Twas there Macbeth lived in days of old,
And a great tyrant he was, be it told.

I wish the Heatherblend members every success,
Hoping God will prosper them and bless;
Long May Dame Fortune smile upon them,
For all of them I've met are kind gentlemen.

And, in conclusion, I must say
I never received better treatment in my day
Than I received from my admirers in bonnie Inverness;
This on my soul and conscience I do confess.

LINES IN PRAISE OF TOMMY ATKINS

Success to Tommy Atkins, he's a very brave man,
And to deny it there's few people can;
And to face his foreign foes he's never afraid,
Therefore he's not a beggar, as Rudyard Kipling has said.

No, he's paid by our Government, and is worthy of his hire;
And from our shores in time of war he makes our foes retire,
He doesn't need to beg; no, nothing so low;
No, he considers it more honourable to face a foreign foe.

No, he's not a beggar, he's a more useful man,
And, as Shakespeare has said, his life's but a span;
And at the cannon's mouth he seeks for reputation,
He doesn't go from door to door seeking a donation.

Oh, think of Tommy Atkins when from home far away,
Lying on the battlefield, earth's cold clay;
And a stone or his knapsack pillowing his head,
And his comrades lying near by him wounded and dead.

And while lying there, poor fellow, he thinks of his wife at
home,
And his heart bleeds at the thought, and he does moan;
And down his cheek flows many a silent tear,
When he thinks of his friends and children dear.

Kind Christians, think of him when far, far away,
Fighting for his Queen and Country without dismay;
May God protect him wherever he goes,
And give him strength to conquer his foes.

To call a soldier a beggar is a very degrading name,
And in my opinion it's a very great shame;
And the man that calls him a beggar is not the soldier's
friend,
And no sensible soldier should on him depend.

A soldier is a man that ought to be respected,
And by his country shouldn't be neglected;
For he fights our foreign foes, and in danger of his life,
Leaving behind him his relatives and his dear wife.

Then hurrah for Tommy Atkins, he's the people's friend,
Because when foreign foes assail us he does us defend;
He is not a beggar, as Rudyard Kipling has said,
No, he doesn't need to beg, he lives by his trade.

And in conclusion I will say,
Don't forget his wife and children when he's far away;
But try and help them all you can,
For remember Tommy Atkins is a very useful man.

THE RELIEF OF MAFEKING

Success to Colonel Baden-Powell and his praises loudly
sing,
For being so brave in relieving Mafeking,
With his gallant little band of eight hundred men,
They made the Boers fly from Mafeking like sheep escaping
from a pen.

'Twas in the year of 1900 and on the 18th of May,
That Colonel Baden-Powell beat the Boers without dismay,
And made them fly from Mafeking without delay,
Which will be handed down to posterity for many a day.

Colonel Baden-Powell is a very brave man,
And to deny it, I venture to say, few men can;
He is a noble hero be it said,
For at the siege of Mafeking he never was afraid.

And during the siege Colonel Baden was cheerful and gay,
While the starving population were living on brawn each
day;
And alas! the sufferings of the women and children were
great,
Yet they all submitted patiently to their fate.

For seven months besieged they fought the Boers without
dismay,
Until at last the Boers were glad to run away;
Because Baden-Powell's gallant band put them to flight
By cannon shot and volleys of musketry to the left and
right.

Then long live Baden-Powell and his brave little band,
For during the siege of Mafeking they made a bold stand
Against yelling thousands of Boers who were thirsting for
their blood,
But as firm as a rock against them they fearlessly stood.

Oh! think of them living on brawn extracted from horse
hides,
While the inhuman Boers their sufferings deride,
Knowing that the women's hearts with grief were torn
As they looked on their children's faces that looked sad and
forlorn.

For 217 days the Boers tried to obtain Mafeking's surrender,
But their strategy was futile owing to its noble defender,
Colonel Baden-Powell, that hero of renown,
Who, by his masterly generalship, saved the town.

Methinks I see him and his gallant band,
Looking terror to the foe: Oh! The sight was really grand,
As he cried, "Give it them, lads; let's do or die;
And from Mafeking we'll soon make them fly,
And we'll make them rue their rash undertaking
The day they laid siege to the town of Mafeking."

Long life and prosperity to Colonel Baden-Powell,
For there's very few generals can him excel;
And he is now the Hero of Mafeking, be it told,
And his name should be engraved on medals of gold.

I wish him and his gallant little band every success,
For relieving the people of Mafeking while in distress;
They made the Boers rue their rash undertaking
The day they laid siege to the town of Mafeking.

For during the defence of Mafeking
From grief he kept the people's hearts from breaking,
Because he sang to them and did recite
Passages from Shakespeare which did their hearts delight.

THE BATTLE OF GLENCOE

Twas in the month of October, and in the year of 1899,
Which the Boers will remember for a very long time,
Because by the British Army they received a crushing blow;
And were driven from Smith's Hill at the Battle of Glencoe.

The Boers' plan of the battle was devised with great skill,
And about 7000 men of them were camped on Smith's Hill;
And at half-past five the battle began,
And the Boers behaved bravely to a man.

At twenty minutes to six two of the British batteries opened fire,
And early in the fight some of the Boers began to retire;
And in half an hour the Boers' artillery had ceased to fire,
And from the crest of the hill they began to retire.

And General Symons with his staff was watching every detail,
The brave hero whose courage in the battle didn't fail;
Because he ordered the King's Royal Rifles and the Dublin Fusiliers,
To advance in skirmishing order, which they did with three cheers.

Then they boldly advanced in very grand style,
And encouraged by their leaders all the while;
And their marching in skirmishing order was beautiful to see,
As they advanced boldly to attack the enemy.

For over an hour the advance continued without dismay,
Until they had to take a breath by the way;
They felt so fatigued climbing up Smith's Hill,
But, nevertheless, the brave heroes did it with a will.

They they prepared to attack the enemy,
And with wild battle-cries they attacked them vigorously;
And with one determined rush they ascended the hill,
And drove the Boers from their position sore against their
will.

But, alas, General Symons received a mortal wound,
Which caused his soldiers' sorrow to be profound;
But still they fought on manfully without any dread;
But, alas, brave General Symons now is dead.

Oh! It was a most inspiring and a magnificent sight,
To see the Hussars spurring their steeds with all their might;
And charging the Boers with their lances of steel,
Which hurled them from their saddles and made them reel.

The battle raged for six hours and more,
While British cannon Smith's Hill up tore;
Still the Boers fought manfully, without dismay,
But in a short time they had to give way.

For the Gordon Highlanders soon put an end to the fight,
Oh! it was a most gorgeous and thrilling sight,
To see them with their bagpipes playing, and one ringing
cheer,
And from Smith's Hill they soon did the Boers clear.

And at the charge of the bayonet they made them fly,
While their leaders cried, "Forward, my lads, do or die,"
And the Boers' blood copiously they did spill,
And the Boers were forced to fly from Smith's Hill.

And in conclusion I hope and pray
The British will be successful when from home far away;
And long may the Gordons be able to conquer the foe,
At home or abroad, wherever they go.

THE CAPTURE OF HAVANA

'Twas in the year 1762 that France and Spain
Resolved, allied together, to crush Britain;
But the British Army sailed from England in May,
And arrived off Havana without any delay.

And the British Army resolved to operate on land,
And the appearance of the British troops were really grand;
And by the Earl of Albermarle the British troops were
  commanded,
All eager for to fight as soon as they were landed.

Arduous and trying was the work the British had to do,
Yet with a hearty goodwill they to it flew;
While the tropical sun on them blazed down,
But the poor soldiers wrought hard and didn't frown.

The bombardment was opened on the 30th of June,
And from the British battleships a fierce cannonade did
boom;
And continued from six in the morning till two o'clock in
the afternoon,
And with grief the French and Spaniards sullenly did
gloom.

And by the 26th of July the guns of Fort Moro were
destroyed,
And the French and Spaniards were greatly annoyed;
Because the British troops entered the Fort without dismay,
And drove them from it at the bayonet charge without
delay.

But for the safety of the city the Governor organised a night
attack,
Thinking to repulse the British and drive them back;
And with fifteen hundred militia he did the British attack,
But the British trench guards soon drove them back.

Then the Spandiards were charged and driven down the
hill,
At the point of the bayonet sore against their will;
And they rushed to their boats, the only refuge they could
find,
Leaving a trail of dead and wounded behind.

Then Lieutenant Forbes, at the head of his men,
Swept round the ramparts driving all before them;
And with levelled bayonets they drove them to and fro,
Then the British flag was hoisted over the bastions of
Moro.

Then the Governor of the castle fell fighting sword in hand,
While rallying his men around the flagstaff the scene was
grand;
And the Spaniards fought hard to save their ships of war,
But the British destroyed their ships and scattered them
afar.

And every man in the Moro Fort was bayonet or shot,
Which in Spanish history will never be forgot;
And on the 10th of August Lord Albemarle sent a flag of
truce,
And summoned the Governor to surrender, but he seemed to
refuse.

Then from the batteries the British opened a terrific fire,
And the Spaniards from their guns were forced to retire,
Because no longer could they the city defend;
Then the firing ceased and hostilities were at an end.

Then the city of Havana surrendered unconditionally,
And terms were settled, and the harbour, forts, and city,
With a district of one hundred miles to the westward,
And loads of gold and silver were the British troops' reward.

And all other valuable property was brought to London,
The spoils that the British Army had won;
And it was conveyed in grand procession to the Tower of
London,
And the Londoners applauded the British for the honours
they had won.

THE BATTLE OF WATERLOO

'Twas in the year 1815, and on the 18th day of June,
That British cannon, against the French army, loudly did
boom,
Upon the ever memorable bloody field of Waterloo;
Which Napoleon remembered while in St Helena, and
bitterly did rue.

The morning of the 18th was gloomy and cheerless to behold,
But the British soon recovered from the severe cold
That they had endured the previous rainy night;
And each man prepared to burnish his arms for the coming fight.

Then the morning passed in mutual arrangements for battle,
And the French guns, at half-past eleven, loudly did rattle;
And immediately the order for attack was given,
Then the bullets flew like lightning till the Heaven's seemed
riven.

The place from which Bonaparte viewed the bloody field
Was the farmhouse of La Belle Alliance, which some
protection   tectiond yield;
And there he remained for the most part of the day,
Pacing to and fro with his hands behind him in doubtful
dismay.

The Duke of Wellington stood upon a bridge behind La Haye,
And viewed the British army in all their grand array,
And where danger threatened most the noble Duke was
found
In the midst of shot and shell on every side around.

Hougemont was the key of the Duke of Wellington's position,
A spot that was naturally very strong, and a great acqusition
To the Duke and his staff during the day,
Which the Coldstream Guards held to the last, without
dismay.

The French 2nd Corps were principally directed during the day
To carry Hougemont farmhouse without delay;
So the farmhouse in quick succession they did attack,
But the British guns on the heights above soon drove them
back.

But still the heavy shot and shells ploughed through the
walls;
Yet the brave Guards resolved to hold the place no matter
what befalls;
And they fought manfully to the last, with courage
unshaken,
Until the tower of Hougemont was in a blaze but still it
remained untaken.

By these desperate attacks Napoleon lost ten thousand men,
And left them weltering in their gore like sheep in a pen;
And the British lost one thousand men — which wasn't very
great,
Because the great Napoleon met with a crushing defeat.

The advance of Napoleon on the right was really very fine,
Which was followed by a general onset upon the British line,
In which three hundred pieces of artillery opened their
cannonade;
But the British artillery played upon them, and great
courage displayed.

For ten long hours it was a continued succession of attacks;
Whilst the British cavalry charged them in all their drawbacks;
And the courage of the British Army was great in square at
Waterloo,
Because hour after hour they were mowed down in numbers
not a few.

At times the temper of the troops had very nearly failed,
Especially amongst the Irish regiments who angry railed;
And they cried: "When will we get at them? Show us the
way
That we may avenge the death of our comrades without
delay?"

"But be steady and cool, my brave lads," was their officers'
command,
While each man was ready to charge with gun in hand;
Oh, Heaven! it was pitiful to see their comrades lying
around,
Dead and weltering in their gore, and cumbering the
ground.

It was a most dreadful sight to behold,
Heaps upon heaps of dead men lying stiff and cold;
While the cries of the dying was lamentable to hear;
And for the loss of their comrades many a soldier shed
a tear.

Men and horses fell on every side around,
Whilst heavy cannon shot tore up the ground;
And musket balls in thousands flew,
And innocent blood bedewed the field of Waterloo.

Methinks I see the solid British square,
Whilst the shout of the French did rend the air,
As they rush against the square of steel.
Which forced them back and made them reel.

And when a gap was made in that square,
The cry of "Close up! Close up!" did rend the air,
"And charge them with your bayonets, and make them fly!
And Scotland for ever! be the cry."

The French and British closed in solid square,
While the smoke of the heavy cannonade darkened the air;
Then the noble Picton deployed his division into line,
And drove back the enemy in a very short time.

Then Lord Anglesey seized on the moment, and charging
with the Greys,
Whilst the Inniskillings burst through everything, which
they did always;
Then the French infantry fell in hundreds by the swords of
the Dragoons;
Whilst the thundering of the cannonade loudly booms.

And the Eagles of the 45th and 105th were all captured that
day,
And upwards of 2000 prisoners, all in grand array;
But, alas! at the head of his division, the noble Picton fell,
While the Highlanders played a lament for him they loved
so well.

Then the French cavalry receded from the square they
couldn't penetrate,
Still Napoleon thought to weary the British into defeat;
But when he saw his columns driven back in dismay,
He cried, "How beautifully these English fight, but they
must give way."

And well did British bravery deserve the proud encomium,
Which their enduring courage drew from the brave Napoleon;
And when the close column of infantry came on the British
square,
Then the British gave one loud cheer which did rend the air.

Then the French army pressed forward at Napoleon's
command,
Determined, no doubt, to make a bold stand;
Then Wellington cried, "Up Guards and break their ranks
through,
And chase the French invaders from off the field of Waterloo!"

Then, in a moment, they were all on their feet,
And they met the French, sword in hand, and made them
retreat;
Then Wellington in person directed the attack,
And at every point and turning the French were beaten
back.

And the road was choked and encumbered with the dead;
And, unable to stand the charge, the French instantly fled,
And Napoleon's army of yesterday was now a total wreck,
Which the British manfully for ten long hours held in check.

Then, panic-struck, the French were forced to yield,
And Napoleon turned his charger's head, and fled from the
field,
With his heart full of woe, no doubt—
Exclaiming, "Oh, Heaven! my noble army has met with a
total rout!"

THE ALBION BATTLESHIP CALAMITY

'Twas in the year of 1898, and on the 21st of June,
The launching of the Battleship Albion caused a great
gloom,
Amongst the relatives of many persons who were drowned
in the River Thames,
Which their relatives will remember while life remains.

The vessel was christened by the Duchess of York,
And the spectators' hearts felt as light as cork
As the Duchess cut the cord that was holding the fine ship,
Then the spectators loudly cheered as the vessel slid down
the slip.

The launching of the vessel was very well carried out,
While the guests on the stands cheered without any
doubt,
Under the impression that everything would go well;
But, alas! instantaneously a bridge and staging fell.

Oh! little did the Duchess of York think that day
That so many lives would be taken away
At the launching of the good ship Albion,
But when she heard of the catastrophe she felt woebegone.

But accidents will happen without any doubt,
And often the cause thereof is hard to find out;
And according to report, I've heard people say,
'Twas the great crowd on the bridge caused it to give
way.

Just as the vessel entered the water the bridge and staging
gave way,
Immersing some three hundred people which caused great
dismay
Amongst thousands of spectators that were standing there,
And in the faces of the bystanders were depicted despair.

Then the police boats instantly made for the fatal spot,
And with the aid of dockyard hands several people were
got,
While some scrambled out themselves, the best way they
could—
And the most of them were the inhabitants of the neighbourhood.

Part of them were the wives and daughters of the dockyard
hands,
And as they gazed upon them they in amazement
stands;
And several bodies were hauled up quite dead,
Which filled the onlookers' hearts with pity and dread.

One of the first rescued was a little baby,
Which was conveyed away to a mortuary;
And several were taken to the fitter's shed, and attended to
there
By the firemen and several nurses with the greatest care.

Meanwhile heartrending scenes were taking place,
Whilst the tears ran down many a Mother and Father's
face,
That had lost their children in the River Thames,
Which they will remember while life remains.

Oh, Heaven! it was horrible to see the bodies laid out
in rows,
And as Fathers and Mothers passed along, adown their
cheeks the tears flows,
While their poor, sickly hearts were throbbing with fear.

A great crowd had gathered to search for the missing
dead,
And many strong men broke down because their heart with
pity bled,
As they looked upon the distorted faces of their relatives
dear,
While adown their cheeks flowed many a silent tear.

The tenderest sympathy, no doubt, was shown to them,
By the kind hearted Police and Firemen;
The scene in fact was most sickening to behold,
And enough to make one's blood run cold,
To see tear-stained men and women there
Searching for their relatives, and in their eyes a pitiful
stare.

There's one brave man in particular I must mention,
And I'm sure he's worthy of the people's attention:
His name is Thomas Cooke, of No. 6 Percy Road, Canning
Town,
Who's name ought to be to posterity handed down,
Because he leapt into the River Thames, and heroically did
behave,
And rescued five persons from a watery grave.

Mr Wilson, a young Electrician, got a terrible fright,
When he saw his mother and sister dead — he was shocked at the sight,
Because his sister had not many days returned from her honeymoon,
And in his countenance, alas! there was a sad gloom.

Her Majesty has sent a message of sympathy to the bereaved ones in distress,
And the Duke and Duchess of York have sent 25 guineas I must confess,
And £1000 from the Directors of the Thames Ironworks and Shipbuilding Company,
Which I hope will help to fill the bereaved one's hearts with glee.

And in conclusion I will venture to say,
That accidents will happen by night and by day;
And I will say without any fear,
Because to me it appears quite clear,
That the stronger we our houses do build,
The less chance we have of being killed.

AN ALL NIGHT SEA FIGHT

Ye sons of Mars, come list to me,
And I will relate to ye
A great and heroic naval fight,
Which will fill your hearts with delight.

The fight was between the French Frigate "Pique" and the
British Frigate "Blanche,"
But the British crew were bold and staunch;
And the battle was fought in West Indian waters in the year
of 1795,
And for to gain the victory the French did nobly strive.

And on the morning of the 4th of January while cruising off
Gadulope,
The look-out man from the foretop loudly spoke,
And cried, "Sail ahoy!" "Where away?"
"On the lee bow, close in shore, sir," was answered without
delay.

Then Captain Faulkner cried, "Clear the decks!
And the French vessel with his eyeglass he inspects;
And he told his men to hoist the British flag,
And "prepare my heroes to pull down that French rag."

Then the "Blanche" made sail and bore away
In the direction of the "Pique" without delay;
And Captain Faulkner cried, "Now, my lads, bear down on
him,
And make ready quickly and begin."

It was about midnight when the Frenchman hove in sight,
And could be seen distinctly in the starlight;
And for an hour and a half they fired away
Broadsides into each other without dismay.

And with the rapid flashes the Heavens were aflame,
As each volley from the roaring cannons came;
And the incessant roll of musketry was awful to hear,
As it broke over the silent sea and smote upon the ear.

The French vessel had nearly 400 men,
Her decks were literally crowded from stem to stern;
And the musketeers kept up a fierce fire on the "Blanche,"
But still the "Blanche" on them did advance.

And the "Blanche's" crew without dismay
Fired a broadside into the "Pique" without delay,
Which raked her fore and aft, and knocked her to smash,
And the mizenmast fell overboard with a terrible crash.

Then the Frenchmen rushed forward to board the
"Blanche,"
But in doing so they had a very poor chance,
For the British Tars in courage didn't lack,
Because thrice in succession on their own deck they were
driven back.

Then "Bravo, my lads!" Captain Faulkner loudly cries,
"Lash her bowsprit to our capstan, she's our prize";
And he seized some ropes to lash round his foe,
But a musket ball pierced his heart and laid him low.

Then a yell of rage burst from the noble crew,
And near to his fallen body they drew;
And tears for his loss fell fast on the deck,
Their grief was so great their tears they couldn't check.

The crew was very sorry for their captain's downfall,
But the sight didn't their brave hearts appal;
Because they fastened the ropes to the "Pique" at the
capstan,
And the "Pique" was dragged after the "Blanche," the
sight was grand.

Yet the crew of the "Pique" maintained the fight,
Oh! most courageously they fought in the dead of night;
And for two hours they kept up firing without dismay,
But it was a sacrifice of human life, they had to give way.

And about five o'clock in the morning the French cried for
quarter,
Because on board there had been a great slaughter;
Their Captain Cousail was mortally wounded in the fight
Along with many officers and men; oh! it was a heart-rending
sight
To see the wounded and dead weltering in their gore
After the cannonading had ceased and the fighting was o'er.

WRECK OF THE STEAMER "STELLA"

'Twas in the month of March and in the year of 1899,
Which will be remembered for a very long time;
The wreck of the steamer "Stella" that was wrecked on the
Casquet Rocks,
By losing her bearings in a fog, and received some terrible
shocks.

The "Stella" was bound for the Channel Islands on a holiday
trip,
And a number of passengers were resolved not to let the
chance slip;
And the hearts of the passengers felt light and gay,
As the "Stella" steamed out of the London Docks without
delay.

The vessel left London at a quarter-past eleven,
With a full passenger list and a favourable wind from
heaven;
And all went well until late in the afternoon,
When all at once a mist arose, alas! too soon.

And as the Channel Islands were approached a fog set in,
Then the passengers began to be afraid and made a chattering
din;
And about half-past three o'clock the fog settled down,
Which caused Captain Reeks and the passengers with fear
to frown.

And brave Captain Reeks felt rather nervous and discontent,
Because to him it soon became quite evident;
And from his long experience he plainly did see
That the fog was increasing in great density.

Still the "Stella" sailed on at a very rapid rate,
And, of, heaven! rushed headlong on to her fate,
And passed o'er the jagged rocks without delay,
And her side was ripped open: Oh! horror and dismay!

Then all the passengers felt the terrible shock,
As the "Stella" stuck fast upon the first ledge of rock;
And they rushed to the deck in wild alarm,
While some of them cried: "Oh! God protect us from
harm."

Then men clasped wives and daughters, and friends shook
hands,
And unmoved Captain Reeks upon the bridge stands;
And he shouted, "Get out the boats without delay!"
Then the sailors and officers began to work without dismay.

Again Captain Reeks cried in a manly clear voice,
"Let the women and children be our first choice!
Then the boats were loaded in a speedy way,
And with brave seamen to navigate them that felt no
dismay.

Then the "Stella" began rapidly for to settle down,
And Captain Reeks gave his last order without a frown,
Shouting, "Men, for yourselves, you'll better look out!"
Which they did, needing no second bidding, without fear or
doubt.

Then the male passengers rushed to the boats in wild
despair,
While the cries of the women and children rent the air;
Oh, heaven! such a scene! 'twas enough to make one weep,
To see mothers trying to save their children that were fast
asleep.

Brave Captain Reeks stood on the bridge till the ship went
down,
With his eyes uplifted towards heaven, and on his face no
frown;
And some of the passengers jumped from the ship into the
sea,
And tried hard to save their lives right manfully.

But the sufferings of the survivors are pitiful to hear,
And I think all Christian people for them will drop a tear,
Because the rower of the boats were exhausted with damp
and cold;
And the heroine of the wreck was Miss Greta Williams, be it
told.

She remained in an open boat with her fellow-passengers and
crew,
And sang "O rest in the Lord, and He will come to our
rescue";
And for fourteen hours they were rowing on the mighty
deep,
And when each man was done with his turn he fell asleep.

And about six o'clock in the morning a man shrieked out,
"There's a sailing boat coming towards us without any
doubt";
And before the sailing boat could get near, a steamer hove
in sight,
Which proved to be the steamer "Lynx," to their delight.

And they were conveyed to Guernsey without delay,
Poor souls, with their hearts in a state of joy and dismay;
But alas! more than eighty persons have been lost in the
briny deep,
But I hope their souls are now in heaven in safe keep.

WRECK OF THE STEAMER "STORM QUEEN"

Ye landsmen, all pray list to me,
While I relate a terrible tale of the sea,
Concerning the screw steamer "Storm Queen"
Which was wrecked, alas! a most heart-rending scene.

From Sebastopol, with a cargo of grain, she was on her way,
And soon after entering the Bay of Biscay,
On the 21st of December, they experienced a fearful storm
Such as they never experienced since they were born.

The merciless sea was running mountains high,
And to save themselves from a watery grave manfully they
  did try;
But the vessel became unmanageable, but still they worked
  away,
And managed to launch two small boats without dismay.

They wrought most manfully and behaved very well,
But a big wave smashed a small boat before they left the
  vessel;
Still the Captain, Mr Jaques, and five of the crew
Clung to the "Storm Queen" until she sank beneath the
  waters blue.

While the sea lashed itself into white foam and loudly did
  roar,
And with a gurgling sound the big waves covered the vessel
  o'er;
So perished Captain Jaques and five of the crew
Who stuck to the vessel, as brave sailors would do.

But before the vessel sank a raft was made,
And a few men got on to it who were not afraid;
And oh! it was enough to make one's blood to freeze
To see them jumping off the steamer into the yawning
  seas.

So they were tossed about on the big billows the whole
night,
And beneath the big waves they were engulphed before
daylight;
But 22 that reached the boats were saved in all
By the aid of God, on whom they did call.

And on the next morning before daylight
The Norwegian barque "Gulvare" hove in sight;
Then they shouted and pulled towards her with all their
might,
While the seas were running high, oh! what a fearful sight.

The poor souls were prevented from getting along side
Of the barque "Gulvare" by the heavy seas and tide;
And as the boats drew near the barque the storm increases
Until the boats struck against her and were dashed to pieces.

It was almost beyond human efforts with the storm to cope,
But most fortunately they were hauled on board by a rope,
While the big waves did lash the barque all over,
But by a merciful providence they were landed safely at
Dover.

The survivors when rescued were in a destitute state,
But nevertheless they seemed resigned to their fate,
And they thanked God that did them save
Most timely from a cold and watery grave.

And during their stay in Dover they received kind treatment,
For which they, poor creatures, felt very content;
And when they recovered from their ills they met at sea,
The authorities sent them home to their own country.

But as for Captain Jaques, few men like him had been,
Because he couldn't be persuaded to desert the "Storm Queen,"
As he declared he wouldn't leave her whatever did betide;
So the brave hero sank with her beneath the waters wide.

WRECK OF THE "ABERCROMBIE ROBINSON"

'Twas in the year of 1842 and on the 27th of May
That six Companies of the 91st Regiment with spirits light and gay,
And forming the Second Battalion, left Naas without delay,
Commanded by Captain Bertie Gordon, to proceed to the Cape straightaway.

And on the second of June they sailed for the Cape of Good Hope
On board the "Abercrombie Robinson," a vessel with which few vessels could cope;
And in August the 25th they reached Table Bay,
Where a battalion of the 91st was warned for service without delay.

To relieve the 91st, which was to be stationed at Cape Town,
An order which the 91st obeyed without a single frown;
And all the officers not on duty obtained leave to go ashore,
Leaving only six aboard, in grief to deplore.

There were 460 men of the 91st seemingly all content,
Besides a draft of the Cape Mounted Rifles and a draft of
the 27th Regiment;
But, alas an hour after midnight on the same night
A strong gale was blowing, which filled the passengers'
hearts with fright.

The ship pitched heavily and could be felt touching the
ground,
Then Captain Gordon warned the Sergeant-Major and officers
all round,
That they might expect a storm, to him it seemed plain;
And, as he predicted, it blew a terrific hurricane.

And the passengers' hearts were filled with dismay,
And a little after three o'clock in the morning the cable
broke away,
Then the ship drifted helplessly before the merciless storm,
While the women and children looked sad, pale and
forlorn.

Then the thunder roared and the lightning flashed in bright
array,
And was one of the greatest storms ever raged over Table
Bay,
And the ill-fated vessel drove in towards the shore,
While the Storm Fiend did laugh and loudly did roar.

And the ship rolled and heaved with the raging tide,
While the seas poured down the hatchways and broke over
her side,
And the ship wrought for herself a bed in the sand;
Still Captain Bertie hoped all might get safely to land.

'Twas about seven o'clock when daylight did appear,
And when the storm ceases the passengers gave a cheer,
Who had been kept below during the awful night,
Then in small groups they came on deck, a most pitiful
sight.

Alas! sad and dejected, sickly looking, pale and forlorn,
Owing to the close confinement during the storm;
And for a time attempts were made to send a rope
ashore,
But these proved futile owing to the raging billows which
loudly did roar.

Then one of the ship's cutters was carefully lowered over
the side,
And her crew towards the shore merrily did glide,
And succeeded in reaching the shore with a leading line,
And two boats were conveyed to the sinking ship just in
time.

And to save the women and children from being drowned,
Captain Gordon gave orders to the 91st all round
For the women and children to disembark immediately,
Who to God were crying for help most frantically.

And the 91st made a most determined stand.
While lowering the women and children it was awful and
grand,
As they lowered them gently into the boats over the ship's
side,
Regardless of their own lives whatever would betide.

Then the sick were to disembark after the women and
children,
And next the 27th Regiment and Cape Mounted Riflemen;
And from half-past eight till ten o'clock the disembarkation
went on,
While the women and children looked ghastly pale and woe
begone.

The disembarkation of the 91st came at last,
And as there were only two boats available they stood
aghast,
Because the boats only carried each time thirty;
Still, the work went on for four hours most manfully.

And at half-past three the last boat left the ship's side,
And o'er the raging billows the small boats did glide,
Containing the officers and crew who remained to the last,
To see the women and children saved and all danger past.

And after a night of great danger and through a raging sea
Seven hundred souls were carried from a sinking ship providentially;
And among them were trembling children and nervous
women also,
And sick men who were dying with their hearts full of woe.

But thank God they were all saved and brought to land,
All through Colonel Bertie Gordon, who wisely did command
The 91st to see to the women and children's safety,
An order which they obeyed right manfully;
And all honour is due to the 91st for their gallantry,
Likewise Captain Bertie Gordon, who behaved so heroically.

LOSS OF THE "VICTORIA"

Alas! Now o'er Britannia there hangs a gloom,
Because over 400 British Tars have met with a watery tomb;
Who served aboard the "Victoria," the biggest ship in the
navy,
And one of the finest battleships that ever sailed the sea.

And commanded by Sir George Tyron, a noble hero bold,
And his name on his tombstone should be written in letters
of gold;
For he was skifull in naval tactics, few men could with him
cope,
And he was considered to be the nation's hope.

'Twas on Thursday, She twenty-second of June,
And off the coast of tyria, and in the afternoon,
And in the year of our Lord eighteen ninety-three,
That the ill-fated "Victoria" sank to the bottom of the sea.

The "Victoria" sank in fifteen minutes after she was rammed,
In eighty fathoms of water, which was smoothly calmed;
The monster war vessel capsized bottom uppermost,
And, alas, lies buried in the sea totally lost.

The "Victoria" was the flagship of the Mediterranean Fleet,
And was struck by the "Camperdown" when too close they
did meet,
While practising the naval and useful art of war,
How to wheel and discharge their shot at the enemy
afar.

Oh, Heaven! Methinks I see some men lying in their
beds,
And some skylarking, no doubt, and not a soul dreads
The coming avalanche that was to seal their doom,
Until down came the mighty fabric of the engine room.

Then death leaped on them from all quarters in a moment,
And there were explosions of magazines and boilers rent;
And the fire and steam and water beat out all life,
But I hope the drowned ones are in the better world free
from strife.

Sir George Tyron was on the bridge at the moment of the
accident
With folded arms, seemingly quite content;
And seeing the vessel couldn't be saved he remained till the last,
And went down with the "Victoria" when all succour was
past.

Methinks I see him on the bridge like a hero brave,
And the ship slowly sinking into the briny wave;
And when the men cried, "Save yourselves without
delay,"
He told them to save themselves, he felt no dismay.

'Twas only those that leaped from the vessel at the first
alarm,
Luckily so, that were saved from any harm
By leaping into the boats o'er the vessel's side,
Thanking God they had escaped as o'er the smooth water
they did glide.

At Whitehall, London, mothers and fathers did call,
And the pitiful scene did the spectators' hearts appal;
But the most painful case was the mother of J.P. Scarlet,
Who cried, "Oh, Heaven, the loss of my son I'll never
forget."

Oh, Heaven! Befriend the bereaved ones, hard is their fate,
Which I am sorry at heart to relate;
But I hope God in His goodness will provide for them,
Especially the widows, for the loss of their men.

Alas! Britannia now will mourn the loss of her naval
commander,
Who was as brave as the great Alexander;
And to his honour be it fearlessly told,
Few men would excel this hero bold.

Alas! 'Tis sad to be buried in eighty fathoms of Syrian sea,
Which will hide the secret of the "Victoria" to all eternity;
Which causes Britannia's sorrow to be profound
For the brave British Tars that have been drowned.

BURNING OF THE SHIP "KENT"

Good people of high and low degree,
I pray ye all to list to me,
And I'll relate a harrowing tale of the sea
Concerning the burning of the ship "Kent" in the Bay of
Biscay,
Which is the most appalling tale of the present century.

She carried a crew, including officers, of 148 men,
And twenty lady passengers along with them;
Besides 344 men of the 31st Regiment,
And twenty officers with them, all seemingly content.

Also the soldiers' wives, which numbered forty-three,
And sixty-six children, a most beautiful sight to see;
And in the year of 1825, and on the 19th of February,
The ship "Kent" sailed from the Downs right speedily,
While the passengers' hearts felt light with glee.

And the beautiful ship proceeded on her way to Bengal,
While the passengers were cheerful one and all;
And the sun shone out in brilliant array,
And on the evening of the 28th they entered the Bay of
Biscay.

But a gale from the south-west sprang up that night,
Which filled the passengers' hearts with fright;
And it continued to increase in violence as the night wore on,
Whilst the lady passengers looked very woe-begone.

Part of the cargo in the hold consisted of shot and shell,
And the vessel rolled heavily as the big billows rose and fell;
Then two sailors descended the forehold carrying a light,
To see if all below was safe and right.

And they discovered a spirit cask and the contents oozing
rapidly,
And the man with the light stooped to examine it
immediately;
And in doing so he dropped the lamp while in a state of
amaze,
And, oh horror! in a minute the forehold was in a blaze.

It was two o'clock in the morning when the accident took
  place,
And, alas! horror and fear was depicted in each face;
And the sailors tried hard to extinguish the flame,
But, oh Heaven! all their exertions proved in vain.

The inflammable matter rendered their efforts of no avail,
And the brave sailors with over-exertion looked very pale;
And for hours in the darkness they tried to check the fire,
But the flames still mounted higher and higher.

But Captain Cobb resolved on a last desperate experiment,
Because he saw the ship was doomed, and he felt discontent;
Then he raised the alarm that the ship was on fire,
Then the passengers quickly from their beds did retire.

And women and children rushed to the deck in wild despair,
And, paralyed with terror, many women tore their hair;
And some prayed to God for help, and wildly did screech,
But, alas! poor souls, help was not within their reach.

Still the gale blew hard, and the waves ran mountains high,
While men, women, and children bitterly did cry
To God to save them from the merciless fire;
But the flames rose higher and higher.

And when the passengers had lost all hope, and in great
  dismay,
The look-out man shouted, "Ho! a sail coming this way";
Then every heart felt light and gay,
And signals of distress were hoisted without delay.

Then the vessel came to their rescue, commanded by Captain
Cook,
And he gazed upon the burning ship with a pitiful look;
She proved to be the brig "Cambria," bound for Vera Cruz,
Then the captain cried, "Men, save all ye can, there's no
time to lose."

Then the sailors of the "Cambria" wrought with might and
main,
While the sea spray fell on them like heavy rain;
First the women and children were transferred from the
"Kent"
By boats, ropes, and tackle without a single accident.

But, alas! the fire had reached the powder magazine,
Then followed an explosion, oh! what a fearful scene;
But the explosion was witnessed by Captain Babby of the
ship "Carline,"
Who most fortunately arrived in the nick of time.

And fourteen additional human beings were saved from the
"Kent,"
And they thanked Captain Babby and God, who to them
succour sent,
And had saved them from being burnt, and drowned in the
briny deep;
And they felt so overjoyed that some of them did weep;
And in the first port in England they landed without delay,
And when their feet touched English soil their hearts felt
gay.

WRECK OF THE "INDIAN CHIEF"

'Twas on the 8th of January 1881,
That a terrific gale along the English Channel ran,
And spread death and disaster in its train,
Whereby the "Indian Chief" vessel was tossed on the raging main.

She was driven ashore on the Goodwin Sands,
And the good captain fearlessly issued his commands,
"Come, my men, try and save the vessel, work with all your
might,"
Although the poor sailors on board were in a fearful plight.

They were expecting every minute her hull would give way,
And they, poor souls, felt stricken with dismay,
And the captain and some of the crew clung to the main masts,
Where they were exposed to the wind's cold blasts.

A fierce gale was blowing and the sea ran mountains high,
And the sailors on board heaved many a bitter sigh;
And in the teeth of the storm the lifeboat was rowed bravely
Towards the ship in distress, which was awful to see.

The ship was lifted high on the crest of a wave,
While the sailors tried hard their lives to save,
And implored God to save them from a watery grave,
And through fear some of them began to rave.

The waves were miles long in length,
And the sailors had lost nearly all their strength,
By striving hard their lives to save,
From being drowned in the briny wave.

A ration of rum and a biscuit was served out to each man,
And the weary night passed, and then appeared the morning
dawn;
And when the lifeboat hove in sight a sailor did shout,
"Thank God, there's she at last without any doubt."

But, with weakness and the biting cold,
Several of the sailors let go their hold;
And, alas, fell into the yawning sea,
Poor souls! and were launched into eternity.

Oh, it was a most fearful plight,
For the poor sailors to be in the rigging all night;
While the storm fiend did laugh and roar,
And the big waves lashed the ship all o'er.

And as the lifeboat drew near,
The poor sailors raised a faint cheer;
And all the lifeboat men saw was a solitary mast,
And some sailors clinging to it, while the ship was sinking
fast.

Charles Tait, the coxswain of the lifeboat, was a skilful
boatman,
And the bravery he and his crew displayed was really grand;
For his men were hardy and a very heroic set,
And for bravery their equals it would be hard to get.

But, thank God, out of twenty-nine eleven were saved,
Owing to the way the lifeboat men behaved;
And when they landed with the eleven wreckers at Ramsgate,
The people's joy was very great.

DEATH OF CAPTAIN WARD

'Twas about the beginning of the past century
Billy Bowls was pressed into the British Navy,
And conveyed on board the "Waterwitch" without delay,
Scarce getting time to bid farewell to the villagers of Fairway.

And once on board the "Waterwitch" he resolved to do his
duty,
And if he returned safe home he'd marry Nelly Blyth, his
beauty;
And he'd fight for old England like a jolly British tar,
And the thought of Nelly Blyth would solace him during
the war.

Poor fellow, he little thought what he had to go through,
But in all his trials at sea he never did rue;
No, the brave tar became reconciled to his fate,
And felt proud of his commander, Captain Ward the Great.

And on board the "Waterwitch" was Tom Riggles, his old
comrade,
And with such a comrade he seldom felt afraid;
Because the stories they told each other made the time pass
quickly away,
And made their hearts feel light and gay.

'Twas on a Sunday morning and clear to the view,
Captain Ward the attention of his men he drew;
"Look!" he cried, "There's two French men-of-war on
our right,
Therefore prepare, my lads, immediately to begin the fight."

Then the "Waterwitch" was steered to the ship that was
most near,
While every man resolved to sell their lives most dear;
But the French commander disinclined to engage in the
fight,
And he ordered his men to put on a press of canvas and
take to flight.

Then Captain Ward gave the order to fire,
Then Billy Bowls cried, "Now we'll get fighting to our
hearts' desire";
And for an hour a running fight was maintained,
And the two ships of the enemy near upon the "Waterwitch"
gained.

Captain Ward walked the deck with a firm tread,
When a shot from the enemy pierced the ship, yet he felt no
dread;
But with a splinter Bill Bowls was wounded on the left arm,
And he cried, "Death to the frog-eaters, they have doen me
little harm."

Then Captain Ward cried, "Fear not, my men, we will win
the day,
Now, men, pour in a broadside without delay";
Then they sailed around the "St Denis" and the "Gloire,"
And in their cabin windows they poured a deadly fire.

The effect on the two ships was tremendous to behold,
But the Frenchmen stuck to their guns with courage
bold;
And the crash and din of artillery was deafening to the ear,
And the cries of the wounded men were pitiful to hear.

Then Captain Ward to his men did say,
"We must board the Frenchman without delay";
Then he seized his cutlass as he spoke,
And jumped on board the "St Denis" in the midst of the
smoke.

Then Bill Bowls and Tom Riggles hastily followed him,
Then, hand to hand, the battle did begin;
And the men sprang upon their foe and beat them back,
And hauled down their colours and hoisted the Union
Jack.

But the men on board the "St Denis" fought desperately
hard,
And just as the "St Denis" was captured a ball struck
Captain Ward
Right on the forehead, and he fell without a groan,
And for the death of Captain Ward the men did moan.

Then the first lieutenant who was standing near by,
Loudly to the men did cry,
"Come, men, and carry your noble commander below;
But there's one consolation, we have beaten the foe."

And thus fell Captain Ward in the prime of life,
But I hope he is now in the better world free from strife;
But, alas! 'tis sad to think he was buried in the mighty
deep,
Where too many of our brave seamen silently sleep.

DISASTROUS FIRE AT SCARBOROUGH

'Twas in the year of 1898, and on the 8th of June,
A mother and six children met with a cruel doom
In one of the most fearful fires for some years past—
And as the spectators gazed upon them they stood aghast.

The fire broke out in a hairdresser's, in the town of Scarborough,
And as the fire spread it filled the people's hearts with
 sorrow;
But the police and the fire brigade were soon on the ground,
Then the hose and reel were quickly sent round.

Oh! it was horrible to see the flames leaping up all around,
While amongst the spectators the silence was profound,
As they saw a man climb out to the parapet high,
Resolved to save his life, or in the attempt to die!

And he gave one half frantic leap, with his heart full of woe,
And came down upon the roof of a public-house 20 feet
 below;
But, alas! he slipped and fell through the skylight,
And received cuts and bruises: oh, what a horrible sight!

He was the tenant of the premises, Mr Brookes,
And for his wife and family he enquires, with anxious looks,
But no one could tell him, it did appear,
And when told so adown his cheeks flowed many a tear.

He had been sleeping by himself on the second floor,
When suddenly alarmed, he thought he'd make sure,
And try to escape from the burning pile with his life,
And try and save his family and his wife.

The fire brigade played on the first floor with great speed,
But the flames had very inflammable fuel upon which to
 feed,
So that the fire spread with awful rapidity,
And in twenty minutes the building was doomed to the
 fourth storey.

The firemen wrought with might and main,
But still the fire did on them gain,
That it was two hours before they could reach the second
 floor,
The heat being so intense they could scarely it endure.

And inside all the time a woman and six children were there,
And when the firemen saw them, in amazement they did
 stare;
The sight that met their eyes made them for to start—
Oh, Heaven! the sight was sufficient to rend the strongest
 heart.

For there was Mrs Brookes stretched dead on the floor,
Who had fallen in trying her escape for to procure.
She was lying with one arm over her ten months old child,
And her cries for help, no doubt, were frantic and wild;
And part of her arm was burned off as it lay above
The child she was trying to shield, which shows a mother's
 love.

For the baby's flesh was partly uninjured by the flames,
Which shows that the loving mother had endured great
 pain;
It, however, met its death by suffocation,
And as the spectators gazed thereon, it filled their hearts
 with consternation.

The firemen acted heroically, without any dread,
And when they entered the back premises they found the
six children dead;
But Mr Brookes, 'tis said, is still alive,
And I hope for many years he will survive.

Oh, Heaven! it is cruel to perish by fire,
Therefore let us be watchful before to our beds we retire,
And see that everything is in safe order before we fall asleep,
And pray that God o'er us in the night watch will keep.

BURIAL OF MR GLADSTONE, THE GREAT POLITICAL HERO

Alas! the people now do sigh and moan
For the loss of Wm. Ewart Gladstone,
Who was a very great politician and a moral man,
And to gainsay it there's few people can.

'Twas in the year of 1898, and on the 19th of May,
When his soul took its flight for ever and aye,
And his body lies interred in Westminster Abbey;
But I hope his soul has gone to that Heavenly shore,
Where all trials and troubles cease for evermore.

He was a man of great intellect and genius bright,
And ever faithful to his Queen by day and by night,
And always foremost in a political fight;
And for his services to mankind, God will him requite.

The funeral procession was affecting to see,
Thousands of people were assembled there, of every degree;
And it was almost eleven o'clock when the procession left
  Westminster Hall,
And the friends of the deceased were present — physicians
  and all.

A large force of police was also present there,
And in the faces of the spectators there was a pitiful air,
Yet they were orderly in every way,
And newspaper boys were selling publications without delay.

Present in the procession was Lord Playfair,
And Bailie Walcot was also there,
Also Mr Macpherson of Edinboro—
And all seemingly to be in profound sorrow.

The supporters of the coffin were the Earl Rosebery,
And the Right Honourable Earl of Kimberley,
And the Right Honourable Sir W. Vernon he was there,
And His Royal Highness the Duke of York, I do declare.

George Armitstead, Esq., was there also,
And Lord Rendal, with his heart full of woe;
And the Right Honourable Duke of Rutland,
And the Right Honourable Arthur J. Balfour, on the right
  hand;
Likewise the noble Marquis of Salisbury,
And His Royal Highness the Prince of Wales, of high degree.

And immediately behind the coffin was Lord Pembroke,
The representative of Her Majesty, and the Duke of Norfolk,
Carrying aloft a beautiful short wand,
The insignia of his high, courtly office, which looked very
  grand.

And when the procession arrived at the grave, Mrs Gladstone
was there,
And in her countenance was depicted a very grave air;
And the dear, good lady seemed to sigh and moan
For her departed, loving husband, Wm. Ewart Gladstone.

And on the opposite side of her stood Lord Pembroke,
And Lord Salisbury, who wore a skull cap and cloak;
Also the Prince of Wales and the Duke of Rutland,
And Mr Balfour and Lord Spencer, all looking very bland.

And the clergy were gathered about the head of the grave,
And the attention of the spectators the Dean did crave;
Then he said, "Man that is born of woman hath a short
time to live,
But, Oh, Heavenly Father! do thou our sins forgive."

Then Mrs Gladstone and her two sons knelt down by the grave,
Then the Dean did the Lord's blessing crave,
While Mrs Gladstone and her sons knelt,
While the spectators for them great pity felt.

The scene was very touching and profound,
To see all the mourners bending their heads to the ground,
And, after a minute's most silent prayer,
The leave-taking at the grave was affecting, I do declare.

Then Mrs Gladstone called on little Dorothy Drew,
And immediately the little girl to her grandmamma flew,
And they both left the grave with their heads bowed down,
While tears from their relatives fell to the ground.

Immortal Wm. Ewart Gladstone! I must conclude my muse,
And to write in praise of thee my pen does not refuse—
To tell the world, fearlessly, without the least dismay,
You were the greatest politician in your day.

DEATH OF THE REV. DR WILSON

'Twas in the year of 1888 and on the 17th of January
That the late Rev. Dr Wilson's soul fled away;
The generous-hearted Dr had been ailing for some time,
But death, with his dart, did pierce the heart of the learned
divine.

He was a man of open countenance and of great ability,
And late minister of Free St Paul's Church, Dundee,
And during the twenty-nine years he remained as minister
in Dundee
He struggled hard for the well-being of the community.

He was the author of several works concerning great
men,
In particular the Memoirs of Dr Candlish and Christ turning
His face towards Jerusalem;
Which is well worthy of perusal, I'm sure,
Because the style is concise and the thoughts clear and
pure.

And as for his age, he was in his eightieth year,
And has left a family of one son and five daughters dear,
And for his loss they will shed many a tear,
Because in their hearts they loved him most dear.

He was a man of a very kindly turn,
And many of his old members for him will mourn,
Because as a preacher he was possessed of courage bold,
Just like one of Covenanting heroes of old.

But I hope he is landed safe on Canaan's bright shore,
To sing with bright angels for evermore
Around that golden throne where God's family doth meet
To sing songs night and day, most sacred and sweet.

The coffin containing the remains was brought on Tuesday
evening from Edinboro,
And as the relatives witnessed its departure their hearts
were full of sorrow,
And the remains were laid inside Free St Paul's Church,
Dundee,
And interred on Wednesday in the Western Cemetery.

The funeral service began at half-past one o'clock in the
afternoon,
And with people the church was filled very soon,
And the coffin was placed in the centre of the platform,
And the lid was covered with wreaths which did the coffin
adorn.

There were beautiful wreaths from the grandchildren of the
deceased,
Whom I hope is now from all troubles released
Also there were wreaths from Mrs and Miss Young, Windsor
Street, Dundee,
Which certainly were most beautiful to see.

Besides the tributes of Miss Morrison and Miss H. Morrison
were a beautiful sight,
Also the tributes of Miss Strong and Mr I. martin White,
Also Mrs and the Misses Henderson's, West Park, Dundee,
Besides the Misses White Springrove were magnificent
to see.

The members and office-bearers of the church filled the pews
on the right,
Which was a very impressive and solemn sight;
And psalms and hymns were sung by the congregation,
And the Rev. W. I. Cox concluded the service with great
veneration.

Then the coffin was carried from the church and placed in
the hearse,
While the congregation allowed the friends to disperse,
Then followed the congregation without delay,
Some to join the procession, while others went home
straightaway.

The procession consisted of the hearse and 47 carriages no
less,
Which were drawn up in the Nethergate, I do confess,
And as the cortege passed slowly along the Nethergate,
Large crowds watched the procession and ungrudgingly did
wait.

And when the hearse reached the cemetery the Rev. R.
Waterson offered up a prayer,
Then the coffin was lowered into the grave by the pall-bearers there;
'Twas then the friends began to cry for their sorrow was
profound,
Then along with the people assembled there they left the
burying-ground.

CAPTAIN TEACH *alias* "BLACK BEARD"

Edward Teach was a native of Bristol, and sailed from that
port
On board a privateer, in search of sport,
As one of the crew, during the French War in that station,
And for personal courage he soon gained his Captain's
approbation.

'Twas in the spring of 1717, Captain Harnigold and Teach
sailed from Providence
For the continent of America, and no further hence;
And in their way captured a vessel laden with flour,
Which they put on board their own vessels in the space of
an hour.

They also seized two other vessels and took some gallons of
wine,
Besides plunder to a considerable value, and most of it most
costly design;
And after that they made a prize of a large French Guineaman,
Then to act an independent part Teach now began.

But the news spread throughtout America, far and near,
And filled many of the inhabitants' hearts with fear;
But Lieutenant Maynard with his sloops of war directly
steered,
And left James River on the 17th November in quest of
Black Beard,
And on the evening of the 21st came in sight of the pirate;
And when Black Beard spied his sloops he felt elate.

When he saw the sloops sent to apprehend him,
He didn't lose his courage, but fiendishly did grin;
And told his men to cease from drinking and their tittle-tattle,
Although he had only twenty men on board, and prepare for
battle.

In case anything should happen to him during the engagement,
One of his men asked him, who felt rather discontent,
Whether his wife knew where he had buried his pelf,
When he impiously replied that nobody knew but the devil
and himself.

In the Morning Maynard weighed and sent his boat to sound,
Which, coming near the pirate, unfortunately ran aground;
But Maynard lightened his vessel of the ballast and water,
Whilst from the pirates' ship small shot loudly did clatter.

But the pirates' small shot or slugs didn't Maynard appal,
He told his men to take their cutlasses and be ready upon
his call;
And to conceal themselves every man below,
While he would remain at the helm and face the foe.

Then Black Beard cried, "They're all knocked on the head,"
When he saw no hands upon deck he thought they were dead;
Then Black Beard boarded Maynard's sloop without dismay,
But Maynard's men rushed upon deck, then began the
deadly fray.

Then Black Beard and Maynard engaged sword in hand,
And the pirate fought manfully and made a bold stand;
And Maynard with twelve men, and Black Beard with fourteen,
Made the most desperate and bloody conflict that ever was
seen.

At last with shots and wounds the pirate fell down dead,
Then from his body Maynard severed the pirate's head,
And suspended it upon his bowsprit-end,
And thanked God Who so mercifully did him defend.

Black Beard derived his name from his long black beard,
Which terrified America more than any comet that had ever
appeared;
But, thanks be to God, in this age we need not be afeared,
Of any such pirates as the inhuman Black Beard.

ODE TO THE KING

Oh! God, I thank Thee for restoring King Edward the
Seventh's health again,
And let all his subjects throughout the Empire say Amen;
May God guard him by night and day,
At home and abroad, when he's far away.

May angels guard his bed at night when he lies down,
And may his subjects revere him, and on him do not frown;
May he be honoured by them at home and abroad,
And may he always be protected by the Eternal God.

My blessing on his noble form, and on his lofty head,
May all good angels guard him while living and when dead;
And when the final hour shall come to summons him away,
May his soul be wafted to the realms of bliss I do pray.

Long may he reign, happy and serene,
Also his Queen most beautiful to be seen;
And may God guard his family by night and day,
That they may tread in the paths of virtue and not go astray.

May God prosper King Edward the Seventh wherever he
goes,
May he always reign victorious over his foes;
Long may he be spared to wear the British Crown,
And may God be as a hedge around him at night when he lies down;
May God inspire him with wisdom, and long may be reign
As Emperor of India and King Edward the VII. — Amen.

A SOLDIER'S REPRIEVE

'Twas in the United of America some years ago
An aged father sat at his fireside with his heart full of woe,
And talking to his neighbour, Mr Allan, about his boy
Bennie
That was to be shot because found asleep doing sentinel duty.

"Inside of twenty-four hours, the telegram said,
And, oh! Mr Allan, he's dead, I am afraid.
Where is my brave Bennie now to me is a mystery."
"We will hope with his heavenly Father," said Mr Allan,
soothingly.

"Yes, let us hope God is very merciful," said Mr Allan.
"Yes, yes," said Bennie's father, "my Bennie was a good
man.
He said, 'Father, I'll go and fight for my country.'
'Go, then, Bennie,' I said, 'and God be with ye.'"

Little Blossom, Bennie's sister, sat listening with a blanched
cheek,
Poor soul, but she didn't speak,
Until a gentle tap was heard at the kitchen door,
Then she arose quickly and tripped across the floor.

And opening the door, she received a letter from a neighbour's
hand,
And as she looked upon it in amazement she did stand.
Then she cried aloud, "It is from my brother Bennie.
Yes, it is, dear father, as you can see."

And as his father gazed upon it he thought Bennie was dead,
Then he handed the letter to Mr Allan and by him it was read,
And the minister read as follows: "Dear father, when this
 you see
I shall be dead and in eternity.

"And, dear father, at first it seemed awful to me
The thought of being launched into eternity.
But, dear father, I'm resolved to die like a man,
And keep up my courage and do the best I can.

"You know I promised Jemmie Carr's mother to look after
 her boy,
Who was his mother's pet and only joy.
But one night while on march Jemmie turned sick,
And if I hadn't lent him my arm he'd have dropped very
 quick.

"And that night it was Jemmie's turn to be sentry,
And take poor Jemmie's place I did agree,
But I couldn't keep awake, father, I'm sorry to relate,
And I didn't know it, well, until it was too late.

"Good-bye, dear father, God seems near me,
But I'm not afraid now to be launched into eternity.
No, dear father, I'm going to a world free from strife,
And see my Saviour there in a better, better life,"

That night, softly, little Blossom, Bennie's sister, stole out
And glided down the footpath without any doubt.
She was on her way to Washington, with her heart full of
 woe,
To try and save her brother's life, blow high, blow low.

And when Blossom appeared before President Lincoln,
Poor child, she was looking very woebegone.
Then the President said, "My child, what do you want with me?"
"Please, Bennie's life, sir," she answered timidly.

"Jemmie was sick, sir, and my brother took his place."
"What is this you say, child? Come here and let me see your face."
Then she handed him Bennie's letter, and he read it carefully,
And taking up his pen he wrote a few lines hastily.

Then he said to Blossom, "To-morrow, Bennie will go with you."
And two days after this interview
Bennie and Blossom took their way to their green mountain home,
And poor little Blossom was footsore, but she didn't moan.

And a crowd gathered at the mill depot to welcome them back,
And to grasp the hand of his boy, Farmer Owen wasn't slack,
And tears flowed down his cheeks as he said fervently,
"The Lord be praised for setting my dear boy free."

RICHARD PIGOTT, THE FORGER

Richard Pigott, the forger, was a very bad man,
And to gainsay it there's nobody can,
Because for fifty years he pursued a career of deceit,
And as a forger few men with him could compete.

For by forged letters he tried to accuse Parnell
For the Phoenix Park murders, but mark what befel.
When his conscience smote him he confessed to the fraud,
And the thought thereof no doubt drove him mad.

Then he fled from London without delay,
Knowing he wouldn't be safe there night nor day,
And embarked on board a ship bound for Spain,
Thinking he would escape detection there, but 'twas all in
vain.

Because while staying at a hotel in Spain
He appeared to the landlord to be a little insane.
And he noticed he was always seemingly in dread,
Like a person that had committed a murder and afterwards
fled.

And when arrested in the hotel he seemed very cool,
Just like an innocent schoolboy going to school.
And he said to the detectives, "Wait until my portmanteau
I've got."
And while going for his portmanteau, himself he shot.

So perished Richard Pigott, a forger bold,
Who tried to swear Parnell's life away for the sake of gold,
But the vengeance of God overtook him,
And Parnell's life has been saved, which I consider no sin.

Because he was a man that was very fond of gold,
Not altogether of the miser's craving, I've been told,
But a craving desire after good meat and drink,
And to obtain good things by foul means he never did shrink.

He could eat and drink more than two ordinary men,
And to keep up his high living by foul means we must him condemn,
Because his heart's desire in life was to fare well,
And to keep up his good living he tried to betray Parnell.

Yes, the villain tried hard to swear his life away,
But God protected him by night and by day,
And during his long trial in London, without dismay,
The noble patriot never flinched nor tried to run away.

Richard Pigott was a man that was blinded by his own conceit.
And would have robbed his dearest friend all for good meat,
To satisfy his gluttony and his own sensual indulgence,
Which the inhuman monster considered no great offence.

But now in that undiscovered country he's getting his reward,
And I'm sure few people have for him little regard,
Because he was a villain of the deepest dye,
And but few people for him will heave a sigh.

When I think of such a monster my blood runs cold,
He was like Monteith, that betrayed Wallace for English gold;
But I hope Parnell will prosper for many a day
In despite of his enemies that tried to swear his life away.

Oh! think of his sufferings and how manfully he did stand.
During his long trial in London, to me it seems grand.
To see him standing at the bar, innocent and upright,
Quite cool and defiant, a most beautiful sight.

And to the noble patriot, honour be it said,
He never was the least afraid
To speak on behalf of Home Rule for Ireland,
But like a true patriot nobly he did take his stand.

And may he go on conquering and conquer to the end,
And hoping that God will the right defend,
And protect him always by night and by day,
At home and abroad when far away.

And now since he's set free, Ireland's sons should rejoice
And applaud him to the skies, all with one voice,
For he's their patriot, true and bold,
And an honest, true-hearted gentleman be it told.

THE TROUBLES OF MATTHEW MAHONEY

In a little town in Devonshire, in the mellow September
moonlight,
A gentleman passing along a street saw a pitiful sight,
A man bending over the form of a woman on the pavement.
He was uttering plaintive words and seemingly discontent.

"What's the matter with the woman?" asked the gentleman,
As the poor, fallen woman he did narrowly scan.
"There's something the matter, as yer honour can see,
But it's not right to prate about my wife, blame me."

"Is that really your wife?" said the gentleman.
"Yes, sor, but she looks very pale and wan."
"But surely she is much younger than you?"
"Only fourteen years, sor, that is thrue.

"It's myself that looks a deal oulder nor I really am,
Throuble have whitened my hair, my good gintleman,
Which was once as black as the wings of a crow,
And it's throuble as is dyed it as white as the snow.

Come, my dear sowl, Bridget, it's past nine o'clock,
And to see yez lying there it gives my heart a shock,"
And he smoothed away the raven hair from her forehead,
And her hands hung heavily as if she had been dead.

The gentleman saw what was the matter and he sighed
again,
And he said, "It's a great trial and must give you pain,
But I see you are willing to help her all you can."
But the encouraging words was not lost upon the Irishman.

"Thrial!" he echoed, "Don't mintion it, yer honour,
But the blessing of God rest upon her.
Poor crathur, she's good barrin' this one fault,
And by any one I don't like to hear her miscault."

"What was the reason of her taking to drink?"
"Bless yer honour, that's jest what I oftentimes think,
Some things is done without any rason at all,
And, sure, this one to me is a great downfall.

'Ah, Bridget, my darlin', I never dreamt ye'd come to
this,"
And stooping down, her cheek he did kiss.
While a glittering tear flashed in the moonlight to the ground,
For the poor husband's grief was really profound.

"Have you any children?" asked the gentleman.
"No, yer honour, bless the Lord, contented I am,
I wouldn't have the lambs know any harm o' their mother,
Besides, sor, to me they would be a great bother."

"What is your trade, my good man?"
"Gardening, sor, and mighty fond of it I am.
Kind sor, I am out of a job and I am dying with sorrow."
"Well, you can call at my house by ten o'clock to-morrow.

"And I'll see what I can do for you.
Now, hasten home with your wife, and I bid you adieu.
But stay, my good man, I did not ask your name."
"My name is Matthew Mahoney, after Father Matthew of
great fame."

Then Mahoney stooped and lifted Bridget tenderly,
And carried her home in his arms cheerfully,
And put her to bed while he felt quite content,
Still hoping Bridget would see the folly of drinking and
repent.

And at ten o'clock next morning Matthew was at Blandford Hall,
And politely for Mr Gillespie he did call,
But he was told Mrs Gillespie he would see,
And was invited into the parlour cheerfully.

And when Mrs Gillespie entered the room
She said, "Matthew Mahoney, I suppose you want to
know your doom.
Well, Mathew, tell your wife to call here to-morrow,"
"I'll ax her, my lady, for my heart's full of sorrow."

So Matthew got his wife to make her appearance at Blandford
Hall,
And, trembling, upon Mrs Gillespie poor Bridget did call,
And had a pleasant interview with Mrs Gillespie,
And was told she was wanted for a new lodge-keeper immediately.

"But, Bridget, my dear woman, you musn't drink any more,
For you have got a good husband you ought to adore,
And Mr Gillespie will help you, I'm sure,
Because he is very kind to deserving poor."

And Bridget's repentance was hearty and sincere,
And by the grace of God she never drank whisky, rum, or beer,
And good thoughts come into her mind of Heaven above,
And Matthew Mahoney dearly does her love.

THE PENNSYLVANIA DISASTER

'Twas in the year of 1889, and in the month of June,
Ten thousand people met with a fearful doom,
By the bursting of a dam in Pennsylvania State,
And were burned, and drowned by the flood — oh! pity their
fate!

The embankment of the dam was considered rather weak,
And by the swelled body of water the embankment did break,
And burst o'er the valley like a leaping river,
Which caused the spectators with fear to shiver.

And on rushed the mighty flood, like a roaring big wave,
Whilst the drowning people tried hard their lives to save;
But eight thousand were drowned, and their houses swept
away,
While the spectators looked on, stricken with dismay.

And when the torrent dashed against the houses they
instantly toppled o'er,
Then many of the houses caught fire, which made a terrific roar;
And two thousand people, by the fire, lost their lives,
Consisting of darling girls and boys, also men and their wives.

And when the merciless flood reached Johnstown it was
fifty feet high,
While, in pitiful accents, the drowning people for help did cry;
But hundreds of corpses, by the flood, were swept away,
And Johnstown was blotted out like a child's toy house of clay

Alas! there were many pitiful scenes enacted,
And many parents, for the loss of their children, have gone
distracted,
Especially those that were burned in the merciless flame,
Their dear little ones they will never see again.

And among the sad scenes to be witnessed there,
Was a man and his wife in great despair,
Who had drawn from the burning mass a cradle of their child,
But, oh, heaven! their little one was gone, which almost
drove them wild.

Oh, heaven! it was a pitiful and a most agonising sight,
To see parents struggling hard with all their might,
To save their little ones from being drowned,
But 'twas vain, the mighty flood engulfed them, with a
roaring sound.

There was also a beautiful girl, the belle of Johnstown,
Standing in bare feet, on the river bank, sad and forlorn,
And clad in a loose petticoat, with a shawl over her head,
Which was all that was left her, because her parents were dead.

Her parents were drowned, and their property swept away
with the flood,
And she was watching for them on the bank where she stood,
To see if they would rise to the surface of the water again,
But the dear girl's watching was all in vain.

And as for Conemaugh river, there's nothing could it surpass,
It was dammed up by a wall of corpses in a confused mass;
And the charred bodies could be seen dotting the burning
debris,
While the flames and sparks ascended with a terrific hiss.

The pillaging of the houses in Johnstown is fearful to describe,
By the Hungarians and ghouls, and woe betide
Any person or party that interfered with them,
Because they were mad with drink, and yelling like tigers
in a den.

And many were to be seen engaged in a hand-to-hand fight,
And drinking whisky, and singing wild songs, oh! what a
shameful sight!
But a number of the thieves were lynched and shot
For robbing the dead of their valuables, which will not be
forgot.

Mrs Ogle, like a heroine, in the telegraph office stood at her
post,
And wired words of warning, else more lives would have been
lost;
Besides she was warned to flee, but from her work she
wouldn't stir,
Until at last the merciless flood engulfed her.

And as for the robbery and outrage at the hands of the
ghouls,
I must mention Clara Barton and her band of merciful souls,
Who made their way fearlessly to the wounded in every
street,
And the wounded and half-crazed survivors they kindly did
treat.

Oh, heaven! it was a horrible sight, which will not be forgot,
So many people drowned and burned — oh! hard has been
their lot!
But heaven's will must be done, I'll venture to say,
And accidents will happen until doomsday!

THE SPRIG OF MOSS

THERE lived in Munich a poor, weakly youth,
But for the exact date, I cannot vouch for the truth,
And of seven of a family he was the elder,
Who was named, by his parents, Alois Senefelder.

But, poor fellow, at home his father was lying dead,
And his little brothers and sisters were depending upon him
for bread,
And one evening he was dismissed from his employment,
Which put an end to all his peace and enjoyment.

The poor lad was almost mad, and the next day
His parent's remains to the cemetery were taken away;
And when his father was buried, distracted like he grew,
And he strolled through the streets crying, What shall
I do!

And all night he wandered on sad and alone,
Until he began to think of returning home,
But, to his surprise, on raising his head to look around,
He was in a part of the country which to him was unknown
ground.

And when night came on the poor lad stood aghast,
For all was hushed save the murmuring of a river which
flowed past;
And the loneliness around seemed to fill his heart with awe,
And, with fatigue, he sat down on the first stone he saw.

And there resting his elbows and head on his knees,
He sat gazing at the running water, which did him please;
And by the light of the stars which shone on the water blue,
He cried, I will drown myself, and bid this harsh world adieu.

Besides, I'm good for nothing, to himself he said,
And will only become a burden to my mother, I'm afraid;
And there, at the bottom of that water, said he
From all my misfortunes death will set me free.

But, happily for Alois, more pious thoughts rushed into his
mind,
And courage enough to drown himself he couldn't find,
So he resolved to go home again whatever did betide,
And he asked forgiveness of his Creator by the river side.

And as he knelt, a few incoherent words escaped him,
And the thought of drowning himself he considered a great
sin,
And the more he thought of it, he felt his flesh creep,
But in a few minutes he fell fast asleep.

And he slept soundly, for the stillnes wasn't broke,
And the day was beginning to dawn before he awoke;
Then suddenly he started up as if in a fright,
And he saw very near him a little stone smooth and white,

Upon which was traced the delicate design of a Sprig of Moss,
But to understand such a design he was at a loss,
Then he recollected the Sprig of Moss lying on the stone,
And with his tears he'd moistened it, but it was gone.

But its imprint was delicately imprinted on the stone;
Then, taking the stone under his arm, he resolved to go home,
Saying, God has reserved me for some other thing,
And with joy he couldn't tell how he began to sing.

And on drawing near the city he met his little brother,
Who told him his uncle had visited his mother,
And on beholding their misery had left them money to buy
  food,
Then Alois cried, Thank God, the news is good!

Then 'twas on the first day after Alois came home,
He began the printing of the Sprig of Moss on the stone;
And by taking the impressions of watch-cases he discovered,
  one day,
What is now called the art of Lithography.

So Alois plodded on making known his great discovery,
Until he obtained the notice of the Royal Academy,
Besides, he obtained a gold Medal, and what was more dear
  to his heart,
He lived to see the wide extension of his art.

And when life's prospects may at times appear dreary to ye,
Remember Alois Senefelder, the discoverer of Lithography,
How God saved him from drowning himself in adversity,
And I hope ye all will learn what the Sprig of Moss teaches ye.

And God that made a way through the Red Sea,
If ye only put your trust in Him, He will protect ye,
And light up your path, and strew it with flowers,
And be your only Comforter in all your lonely hours.